MW00425701

Dean Martin

King of Cool

In60Learning

Copyright © 2018 in60Learning

All rights reserved.

ISBN: 9781980622178

Sign up for the LearningList
to receive

eBooks and Audiobooks

at
www.in60Learning.com
Smarter in 60 minutes.

CONTENTS

1 INTRODUCTION

Elvis Presley was never shy in expressing admiration and adulation for his idol: Dean Martin. Deana Martin wrote in her book about her father, *Memories Are Made of This*, that it was the King of Rock n' Roll who dubbed Dean the "King of Cool." Most entertainers would show bravado about receiving such an honorary title from Elvis, but Dean Martin was not like many of his peers. He was the most humble, unassuming, and unpretentious man in Hollywood.

Dean Martin run the gamut in the entertainment industry: he sold millions of albums, hosted his own successful variety show on NBC for nine years, worked on the big screen with some of the biggest names in Hollywood, and his night club act owned Las Vegas before his pal Frank Sinatra set foot on what would become the Rat Pack's stomping ground.

He was blessed with a sensuous voice, handsome Italian features, a sense of humor, and to top it all off, he was a genuinely kind human being. Those who worked with him claimed had his singing career not taken off he would have made it just fine as a comedian; it came naturally to him. His omnipresent glass of J & B scotch that made him appear "loaded" was just a part of that comedic act. In reality, Dean never showed up to work drunk.

First breaking into the spotlight with his comedic partner Jerry Lewis in the late 1940s, "Martin & Lewis" quickly became the most popular comedic duo in America. Together they performed their stage act all across the country, attracting millions, and made 17 pictures together. When the pair broke-up after 10 years, the split put a dagger in the hearts of their millions of fans.

After the break-up, Dean Martin soared to new heights. He made movies that topped the box-office such as *Some Came Running*, *Rio Bravo*, and *The Young Lions*, released hit songs with Capitol Records, and had the most successful one-man show in Las Vegas, being the first to have his first name only on the marquee: Dino. Later with Frank Sinatra and Sammy Davis, Jr., the three men transcended Vegas, both on stage and in *Ocean's Eleven*.

In a 1983 interview, Dean Martin described his life and success this way: wine, women, and song. He made millions of dollars every year by going out on stage and appearing as himself. And he had a blast through it all. Despite his exuberant personality on stage, the real Dean Martin was much more complex. His friends felt he was always attempting to hide his true self. Even his wife of 20 years, Jeanne, revealed she hardly knew the man who was her husband.

The father of seven children, his heart broke when his son, Dean Paul Martin, died in a plane crash. His friend, Frank Sinatra, tried to bring his pal out of retirement and depression, but the death of Dean Paul marked the eight-year demise of his father.

When Dean Martin died on Christmas Day in 1995, he was no longer Dino Paul Crocetti, the Italian-American boy from Steubenville, Ohio, but Dean Martin the legend. Today his old LPs are once again being sold, and his fans all over the world are listening to his hit songs such as "That's Amore," "Ain't That a Kick in the Head," "Memories Are Made of This," and "You're Nobody 'til Somebody Loves You."

Those who knew Dean loved him because he was who he was and never attempted to put on a false image. Dean Martin is still loved today by a whole new generation of admirers listening to that smooth voice with his ever-present cigarette in hand take them back to a time they will never know but can experience through him. Memories are made of Dean.

2 FROM CROUPIER TO CROONER

"Who'd have thunk it? For a boy from Steubenville, Ohio?"

~ Dean Martin on his astounding success

Dean Martin was about as Italian as a boy from Italian-American Ohio could get. His father, Gaetano Crocetti, came to Ellis Island from Montesilvano, Italy, in 1913. Formerly a farm laborer, he immigrated to Steubenville, Ohio, and took on a whole new profession as a barber.

Steubenville is situated 35 miles west of Pittsburgh and housed a large population of Italian-Americans. Angela Barra was from nearby Fernwood, Ohio. She was a first generation American, her parents having emigrated from Italy. In addition to her strong Italian blood, Angela was educated by German nuns. That firm Catholic faith was something she would instill in her son; Dean's rosary beads were always near him.

Among the skills she learned at the knees of the Catholic nuns was seamstressing. Angela became the most well-known seamstress in the region. She would create her husband's suits, her son's clothes, and the heaps of other's suits or dresses for people around the region who respected her work. Angela was never unemployed.

Angela and Gaetano, whom she gave the name Guy, were married in October 1914 in Steubenville. The bride was 16 years-old and her groom was just 19. Guy continued his career as a barber as he and Angela began a family. In June 1916, their first child, Guglielmo, known to the family as Bill, was born. One year later, on June 7, 1917, Dino Paul Crocetti completed the family.

Young Dino grew-up surrounded by his Italian cousins in Steubenville. The Crocetti-Barra family was a tribe. He was constantly outside playing baseball and bocce ball and was active in the Boy Scouts. With his mother being a devout Catholic, Dino served as an altar boy every Sunday. Until her death on Christmas Day, 1966, Angela would be the most adored and treasured woman in her son's life. His favorite meal would forever be his mother's recipe of pasta fagioli.

Being reared in an Italian household, Dino spoke predominantly Italian until he was five years old, when he was forced to learn English in order to succeed in school. Learning English did not motivate the boy to put much effort into his education. He would skip out of school and go to a local theater called the Olympic and watch his favorite movie genre: westerns. He dreamed of being a cowboy and conquering the Wild, Wild West and making all of the women swoon.

So disenchanted with school was Dino, he claimed the only book he ever picked up to read from cover to cover was *Black Beauty*. Finding the book dismal, he decided he would never give reading another chance. In addition to frequenting the movie house, Dino also haunted the local poolrooms and nightclubs. There, the teenager was with the big boys, drinking, smoking, and using bar language. He also found himself increasingly popular with the ladies and learned how to work his charm with that devilish smile and debonair persona.

Dino had a variety of jobs, one time serving as a milkman, another time a gas station attendant, and he even labored in Ohio's steel mills. He would never forget coming back home after an arduous day's work, coughing up soot, digging it out of his fingernails, and combing it out of his hair. As he went through the day's routine, he thought to himself, "There has to be something better than this."

At the ripe age of 16, Dino decided he had had enough of school and dropped out. To his parent's dismay, he became a welterweight and fought under the name "Kid Crocetti." Dino's days of fighting began on the playground when kids would call him a sissy for always dressing impeccably; they soon discovered he was no sissy. Though he was a skilled fighter, he fought just 18 rounds before hanging up the gloves. The job just did not pay, and he had suffered numerous broken knuckles.

Deciding to live life on the dark side, Dino took a job at a cigar store with a casino in the back. First working as a salesclerk, he moved back into the casino and became a professional croupier, a hobby he would use persistently in life. Relatives saw Dino giving up his future to become a gangster and would eventually land in the electric chair. His mother laughed at their predictions, saying Dino had too much talent to go to waste.

As always, Angela was right. During his nights in the clubs and poolrooms he would frequent, Dino would hop up on stage and sing with local groups. It was apparent from the start he had talent and natural moves to go along with it. Dean saw every Bing Crosby picture that was released. He said he, like Frank Sinatra, copied Bing then evolved into his own style. His vocal hero may have been Bing but Dean would later claim it was from Harry Mills of The Mills Brothers that he acquired his mannerisms and smooth gestures. Both Bing and Harry had an undeniable effect on the launching of Dean's career.

In 1938, Dean was hired to sing with local groups around Steubenville. During this first major gig, Dino Crocetti became Dino Martini, named after a well-known Opera singer named Nino Martini. At the beginning of the 1940s, Dino Martini was brought aboard the Sammy Watkins Orchestra as the lead vocalist. Sammy decided that in order for Dino to become a smash in the States he need a more American name, he told him to drop the "i" and make it Dean Martin.

Feeling overtly confident with his voice and new name, Dean started testing new material during his performances. A natural-born comic, he would get up on stage and crack jokes in between his songs or even about his songs. What made his sense of humor so unique was most of the time he was the butt of his own jokes. It thrilled him to hear the audience hoot and holler at his gags, and at him.

With Dean's professional future appearing bright, he added a little romance. While performing in 1941 in the Vogue Room at the Hollenden Hotel in Cleveland, a 23-year-old Dean locked eyes with an 18-year-old Irish-American Catholic named Elizabeth "Betty" MacDonald. Dean fell fast and hard for Betty, and in a few weeks, he proposed to her. She was mesmerized by his Italian looks and smooth voice and accepted his proposal. They were married in October 1941 in Cleveland Heights. The next morning, the newlyweds were on a bus with the Sammy Watkins band embarking on a 6-week tour.

In December of 1943, Dean got the break of a lifetime when he was asked to follow the act of the famous kid from Hoboken, New Jersey: Frank Sinatra. Frank, an Italian like Dean, was performing at the Riobamba club in New York and was the break-out star of the 1940s. Following Frank, who had traveled with the renowned Tommy Dorsey Band, was intimidating to Dean, but he held his own and received positive reviews. More importantly, he and Frank formed a friendship that would last 50 years. That friendship would change the face of entertainment, but Dean would soon meet the partner that would make him a household name.

3 AMERICA'S FAVORITE STRAIGHT MAN

"The love we had for each other was what made that thing work."

~ *Jerry Lewis on his timeless comedic rapport with Dean*

After the lukewarm reviews he received after opening for Frank Sinatra, unfortunately for Dean, the offer to do gigs for good pay did not start rolling in. Struggling to provide for himself and Betty and their two babies, Craig and Claudia, Dean was desperate. When it did not look like a steady performing job was on the horizon, Dean decided to revert back to an old profession: boxing.

Dean shared a hotel room with six men in New York, including a young comedian named Alan King. Dean's idea to make money was to invite spectators from off the streets into their hotel room, watch him and one of his buddies beat each other up, and fight until one of them finally surrendered. Unsurprisingly, the boxing career that began in a dinky New York hotel room did not take off.

Running out of options, Dean decided to continue pursuing a career in singing, knowing he was gifted with that smooth, silky voice. Persistence paid off, and he was hired to do a 15-minute daily radio program called "On the Air: Songs by Dean Martin." It was not much, but it was something. Luckily, a chance meeting at a New York hotel would change it all for Dean.

It was 1944 when Dean met a mushrooming 18-year-old comic named Jerry Lewis at the Belmont Plaza. The two men hit it off immediately and were soon sharing the same bill at different clubs in New York and New Jersey. A couple of years later, when both were appearing at the Havana-Madrid Club in New York, one critic wrote in his column that if the two put their act together and made a comedic duo they would be a smash hit. That wish would soon become a reality.

In July 1946, Jerry Lewis was performing at the 500 Club in Atlantic City. The lead singer came down with a terrible case of laryngitis and the club's owner, the infamous Skinny D'Amato, asked Jerry if he knew of anyone who could replace him. Without hesitating, Jerry said his pal Dean Martin. Making his case, Jerry told Skinny that Dean was more than just a singer; with Jerry, he also performed comedic skits. Skinny told Jerry that he and Dean had one shot to prove him right or both were out on the streets.

Dean jilted the New York club scene and joined Jerry for the big performance at the 500. On that first night, Dean went on stage and performed three of his songs. Jerry followed with a few of his own recordings and that was the show. Skinny was furious.

Giving the duo another chance, he told them tomorrow night they better deliver those "funny things" Jerry promised or they were both out. The following night, the two were on the stage together for almost three hours, just playing off of each other, and the "Martin & Lewis" team was born.

Years later when he was describing the magnetism of "Martin & Lewis," Dean said, "The appeal was we never looked at the audience. We would work to each other." The charisma was there from the day they met; it was more than just comedic rapport. Jerry respected and looked up to Dean, who was 10 years his senior, and Jerry always said what made their performance so believable for 10 years was that love and admiration. Whatever their formula was, the duo went from just a handful in the audience to performing in front of packed houses.

The pair continued to skyrocket. In the spring of 1948, it seemed "Martin & Lewis" reached the top of the Empire State Building when they were hired to perform at the Copacabana, New York's hottest club. They were such a hit they received a call from Ed Sullivan, asking them to appear on his first ever *Toast of the Town*. After Sullivan came "Mr. Television" Milton Berle calling for "Martin & Lewis" to come onto his *Texaco Star Theatre*. Dean was the straight man, the featly dresser, and the debonair singer. Jerry was the riot, the little brother who jested about everything, including Dean's new and improved nose. As the reviewer had written, together they were unstoppable.

It was only natural for Dean and Jerry's next stop to be "La-La Land" itself: Hollywood. When they were appearing at the incomparable Los Angeles club,

Slapsy Maxie's, they hired two young comedic writers to spruce up their routine. One young man was named Norman Lear. Norman went on to create hit shows such as *All in the Family*, *The Jeffersons*, and *Maude*. Almost as soon as the men touched down at Slapsy's they were signing a 6-year contract with Paramount Pictures and film producer Hal Wallis.

The first picture featuring the comedy team "Martin & Lewis" was 1949's *My Friend Irma*. In only seven years, there would be 16 more films. As always, Dean was the singer and Jerry was the clown. More opportunities continued to pour their way when NBC signed them on to do a weekly radio show predictably called, "The Martin & Lewis Show." Capitol Records also signed them to record albums.

Dean's personal life was also evolving. In 1948, while in Miami performing at the Beachcomber Club, Dean's eyes veered to a young blonde with beautiful blue eyes who was the 1947 Orange Bowl Queen, named Jeanne Biegger. Still married to Betty and now a father of four children, Craig, Claudia, Gail, and baby Deana, Dean faced a crucial decision. Dean decided to leave Betty and pursue the beauty queen he had fallen in love with, the woman he always referred to as "my Jeanne."

Dean and Jeanne were married on September 1, 1949, at the Beverly Hills home of the famous owner of Ciro's nightclub, Herman Hover. Jerry served as best man and his wife, Patti, was also an attendant. From the outset, it was clear to Jeanne her husband was not only married to her but also to Jerry. Their honeymoon was the publicity tour of *My Friend Irma*, and she looked on in envy as the two had a ball with each other and made it seem so effortless.

In the fall of 1950, "Martin & Lewis" were signed by NBC to be monthly hosts on NBC's *Colgate Comedy Hour.* At that time, *Colgate Comedy Hour* was on opposite CBS's invincible Ed Sullivan's *Toast of the Town*, but every time Dean and Jerry hosted the *Colgate Comedy Hour,* they topped Sullivan in the ratings. The crew instantly took a liking to Dean more than Jerry. Dean was naturally a relaxed man who made others feel at ease in his presence, and unlike his counterpart, he never let his temper show. And while Jerry could act funny, Dean was naturally funny. It seemed opposites did attract, but cracks began appearing in the marriage.

By 1952, six years into their partnership, "Martin & Lewis" were the hottest act in show business. Wherever they would appear, pandemonium broke out. The two were shattering records. Dean and Jerry were undertaking exhausting schedules. In Chicago, while appearing at The Chicago Theatre, they performed nine shows a day, which ended up totaling 175 shows in just 21 days. The Paramount in New York only held 4,000 in the audience. Outside, 75,000 people showed up just to see Dean and Jerry. They were bigger than Abbott and Costello.

As they were appearing in more films together and performing on stage, Dean began to feel slighted while appearing as the straight man in the duo. Jerry's roles were growing because he attracted more laughs, and Dean seemed to be shrinking. The rumor around Hollywood was that, without Jerry, Dean would be no one. Though Jerry did little to appease his partner's feelings at the time, he would admit that Dean was "the spine" of "Martin & Lewis."

Dean's growing unhappiness was sensed around

the Paramount lot. In the 1980s, he would call the pictures he made with Jerry "terrible." Not because they were not well received by the public, but because of his roles. Dean felt no challenge going to work on the set. All he had to do was slap Jerry when he made some imprudent remark or repeat what Jerry said then walk out of the scene. Dean felt his talents were being squandered.

His true passion remained singing, and in 1953, his first big single with Capitol, "That's Amore," made an appearance in Dean and Jerry's film, *The Caddy*. The song took off, and it soon became a signature Dean tune. But even as Dean was performing the song live on *The Colgate Comedy Hour*, Jerry upstaged his performance, taking over the camera and zooming in on Dean's face. Dean laughed at the antics but inside he was fuming.

Deciding that he could be more like another Italian singer with a television show, Perry Como, Dean made the decision to focus on singing. He also wanted to break-out of the comedy routine and try his hand at more dramatic acting. He was abandoning "Martin & Lewis." Fans were devastated at the news. Even comedians Jackie Gleason and Lou Costello pleaded with Dean and Jerry to stay together. There was no hope; Dean had made up his mind. Their last appearance was July 25, 1956, 10 years to the day of their first appearance at New York's Copacabana.

It was bittersweet for Dean and Jerry. Jerry later recounted he barely made it through the performance. "Martin & Lewis" were no more; now they were Jerry Lewis and Dean Martin. Many believed Jerry's career would skyrocket and Dean's would sink. For a while, it looked as if they could be right.

Dean Martin

4 THE SUMMIT AT THE SANDS

"The success of the Rat Pack was due to the camaraderie. The guys who work together and kid each other and love each other."

~ *Sammy Davis, Jr.*

Dean's first picture after breaking up with Jerry was a comedy titled *Ten Thousand Bedrooms*. At the box office the movie did not even surpass the film's budget. It was appearing that Dean really was lost without Jerry. One appearance at a hotel in Las Vegas would shake it all up for Dean.

When Dean was hired to appear at the Sands Hotel in Las Vegas, he conjured up a gig that was not at all difficult for him to perform: just being himself. Dean went out on the stage with his glass of J & B blended scotch whisky with a splash of soda and a glowing cigarette. His sense of cool calm radiated to the audience, and they fell in love with the real Dean. He sang so painlessly and no longer had to perform on Jerry's timing. Dean had come into his own as a singer and an entertainer, and he did it by not acting at all.

In the recording studio, Dean was taking off. In 1955, he recorded a song titled, "Memories Are Made of This." The song climbed to the number one slot on the *Billboard* Top 100. It was the first of two of Dean's songs that would reach number one and would always remain one of his favorites. Other hit songs recorded for Capitol Records after his split with Jerry included "Volare," "Return to Me," and "Angel Baby."

With his singing career booming, his film career followed. In 1957, Dean was hired by Twentieth Century-Fox to play a New York playboy turned soldier named Michael Whiteacre. The drama titled *The Young Lions* cast Dean with two of the biggest stars of the day, Montgomery Clift and Marlon Brando. Dean was now acting opposite the heavyweights in Hollywood and proved he could do more than comedy.

A few months later, a role came available for a picture called *Some Came Running*, released by MGM. The role called for an actor who enjoyed drinking, gambling, and women. Frank Sinatra, who was starring in the picture along with Shirley MacLaine, said, "Look no further than my old pal, Dean Martin." Playing Bama Dillert would remain one of Dean's favorite characters; he always said that part was made for him.

The camaraderie between Dean and Frank was evident in *Some Came Running*. Audiences saw two men who genuinely had fun together and seemed to have more in common than Dean and Jerry. With Frank and Dean, there was no competition. Unlike with Jerry, Dean did not have to stand off to the side and watch as his scene was hijacked by a comic routine. But Dean did have one complaint about Frank: he kept him up late. Dean woke-up with the sun every morning to play golf, which was when Frank was going to bed.

While both were Italian, Sinatra was known for his fiery temper, while Dean was never known to raise his voice. One day when Frank and Dean were raising a ruckus during a lunch at the Beverly Hills Hotel, the man at the table next to them complained to management. The manager asked the men to please consider the other customers. This made Frank livid. Dean told Frank to calm down, but Frank ignored his friend's wise advice and went over to the gentleman and punched him, causing cranial damage. He threatened to press charges, but never did. Dean never understood Frank's temperament, but he loved him.

Dean would not be striking out on his own for long. In January 1960, Dean, along with Frank, Sammy Davis, Jr., Joey Bishop, and Peter Lawford, brother-in-law to then Senator John F. Kennedy, made their first appearance at the Sands. Frank wanted the group to be called "The Summit," but that name would not stick with the group for long. When the men performed in Vegas, there was never any script; they went out and ad-libbed. The show brought the audience to their knees in laughter. They were the biggest thing in Vegas.

"The Rat Pack" already had a history in Hollywood. One night in the late 40s after returning to her home in Holmby Hills, the actress Lauren Bacall found her husband, Humphrey Bogart, with a group of friends looking disheveled after returning from Vegas. Upon seeing them, she remarked to the group they looked like a rat pack. The boys became known as the "Holmby Hills Rat Pack." Sinatra was a member of that Pack, but it was his association with Dean, Sammy, Joey, and Peter that he would forever be associated with.

Frank was the leader of the Pack. Dean famously said, "It's Frank's world. We're just livin' in it," but Dean was the star performer. The billboard at the Sands Hotel would at times read "Dean Martin – Maybe Frank – Maybe Sammy." All three were funny, but Dean had the natural timing. He would say a comical line after singing such as, "I'd like to do more for ya, but I'm lucky I remembered these," and the audience would die. Frank would say a similar joke and get a few laughs and would ask incredulously, "Why'd he get more laughs than me?" Dean's secret was he did not try to get laughs or compete with Sammy or Frank or any other performer; he simply was who he was.

When Dean would be performing one of his songs, he would rarely finish the whole song, telling the audience, "If you want to hear the whole song, buy the record." He would make a parody of songs, such as, "You made me love you. You woke me up to do it." And often times, he would begin the song "Mr. Wonderful" with, "Every time I hear a newborn baby cry, I think it's mine." He was the cream of the crop.

1960, the year the Rat Pack started performing in Vegas, was an election year. Frank was a close friend of the Kennedy family and of Peter Lawford's, and he wanted his Pack to stump for Kennedy. Dean, a registered Democrat but apolitical and not close to the Lawford family, reluctantly tagged along. The Rat Pack became known as the "Jack Pack." They performed Frank Sinatra's version of the modified "High Hopes," which became JFK's campaign song. Dean joked if Kennedy were elected Dean would be the obvious choice for the post of Secretary of Liquor.

After Kennedy was elected in November 1960, Dean was invited to perform at one of the Inaugural balls, but there was a major issue that prevented him from doing so. Because he had recently married a white Swede named May Britt, Sammy was not invited. Insulted by his friend's snub, Dean backed out of the appearance. After that incident, he had little to do with the Kennedy family but shared the nation's grief when the president was slain in 1963 at the age of 46.

The Rat Pack racked up motion pictures along with their unceasing Vegas acts. Some of the movies included, *Robin and the 7 Hoods*, *Four for Texas*, *Sergeants 3*, and the most legendary of them all, *Ocean's Eleven*. From 1960 to 1964, Dean himself appeared in 15 motion pictures. He tried his hand at musicals like *The Bells Are Ringing* with Judy Holliday and his favorite genre, westerns, such as *Rio Bravo* with "the Duke" himself, John Wayne, and Angie Dickinson.

In 1962, Dean was signed with 20th Century Fox to make a picture with an old friend of his called *Something's Got to Give*. The old friend was none other than Marilyn Monroe. Marilyn was at a fragile stage in life. Abusing sleeping pills and tranquilizers, she would show up to the set late and easily forgot her lines. Dean was patient with her; he adored her, but the picture was lagging behind schedule.

When the studio threatened to fire and replace Marilyn, Dean sued. Eventually, they agreed to continue with the picture, but it was never completed. When Marilyn died in August 1962 at 36, Dean was planning on serving as a pallbearer, but when Joe DiMaggio said no celebrities were allowed at her funeral, that included him. It broke Dean's heart he could not be there for his friend who had seemed so vulnerable yet so sweet.

Despite his hectic schedule in Vegas and in Hollywood, Dean was one of the most dedicated family men in "Tinsel Town." He was an omnipresent parent in the formative years of his seven children, the four from his marriage to Betty and three with Jeanne: Dean Paul, Ricci, and Gina. Jeanne made one request of him: that he be home every night for dinner. He never disappointed her nor his children.

Deana Martin recounted a normal day with her father in her 2004 book. When he arrived home from the studio, he walked into the kitchen to grab a piece of Wonder Bread and make a little sandwich, then carried it into the living room to watch TV. Jeanne would come in and fix him and her a drink and they would spend some alone time together. Before dinner, his children had half an hour to play with him and climb all over him like a jungle gym. After the family dinner, they would play games together or screen a movie. Typical American family.

The early 60s were hot for Dean in the recording studio as well. In 1960, Sinatra formed a recording label called "Reprise." Along with Sinatra, Sammy Davis, Jr., Bing Crosby, Jo Stafford, and many others, Dean joined the ranks of recording artists lending their voice to Sinatra's label. In 1964, his record *Dream with Dean* debuted the hit song "Everybody Loves Somebody."

Originally written in 1947, "Everybody Loves Somebody" had been performed by an array of singers, including Frank, but was not met with particular rave. Dean's version knocked The Beatles off of *Billboard*'s number one slot and became his theme song. In the next two years, Dean would record seven gold records. He was the most in-demand performer in Hollywood and in Vegas.

5 KING OF VARIETY

"I don't remember any performer being so instantly loved as Dean."

~ *Joey Bishop*

Dean Martin was riding high in the mid-1960s thanks to the success of the Rat Pack and the abundant number of pictures he was appearing in. Dean thought he had reached the pinnacle when he was invited to seal his place in entertainment history by putting his hands and footprints at Grauman's Chinese Theater in March 1964.

Due to his popularity, Dean was invited to be on all of the variety shows on the major networks. He made a few appearances as host of ABC's *The Hollywood Palace*, including one memorable show with the young British rock brand, The Rolling Stones. With ratings soaring the nights Dean would appear on the show, ABC offered Dean his own variety show. Soon, CBS and NBC were following their rival network's lead with offers.

Dean was not keen about taking on his own show and dedicating more time to work, which meant less time for golf and his family, which was beginning to include grandchildren. Thinking the networks would not accept this offer, he proposed he would do a show only on the terms he would come in one day a week and film the show, no rehearsals. Knowing they would be crazy to pass-up Dean Martin, NBC accepted his terms.

On Thursday, September 16, 1965, *The Dean Martin Show* aired on NBC. Dean opened his show every week to "Everybody Loves Somebody" with his accompanist and sidekick whom he had known since the early days in Vegas, Ken Lane. According to the show's director, Greg Garrison, the first few shows consisted of some jugglers, a monkey act, a couple singers who had been off the charts for years, and Dean singing a few of his songs. The ratings were a disappointment. Needing to improve the show's standards, Dean asked Garrison to step-up as producer. Garrison did not have to think hard about what he believed the secret to the show's success would be: just let Dean be Dean.

Garrison also used Dean's good looks and love of pretty women to the show's advantage, with the approval of Jeanne. A company of gorgeous young women called "The Golddiggers" were added to the show. "The Golddiggers" gave Dean funny antics to work off of, as he had with Jerry and the Rat Pack, except now there was a touch of sex. In the company of "The Golddiggers," Dean was in heaven.

Dean's method of rehearsing for his weekly television show was virtually no rehearsal at all. To many of his weekly guest stars, this method was ad absurdum. For a star like Lucille Ball who was a consummate professional and swore by rehearsing, working with Dean made them a nervous wreck. Despite the lack of rehearsal, Dean did not come in wandering on filming day. Often, Garrison would read the script with that week's guest stars and Dean would be sitting in his dressing room, watching rehearsals on a TV screen.

Years later, Dean underscored the notion that he did not rehearse at all. In fact, he claimed to rehearse more than the other cast and crew. Yet his rehearsal did not entail physically rehearsing. Each week, three audio cassette tapes were made, with one of the crew reading Dean's lines. Dean would have a tape to listen to at home, one to carry with him while he was golfing, and one for the car. When he went into the studio, some of the crew, not knowing about the tapes, were flabbergasted at how he knew all his lines without having been there the whole week to rehearse. They thought he was brilliant.

The lack of rehearsal seemed to be a common theme for kings of variety. Jackie Gleason was also known to be a man of little preparation. Yet for both men, the ad-libbing always worked in their favor. Dean was rarely able to maintain a straight-face. When comedian Bob Newhart made an appearance and was playing a man trying to return a toupee his wife bought him for their anniversary because it kept falling off into places like cheese dip, Dean grew hysterical as Bob delivered his dialogue. On the air, he said to Dean, "Are you sure you worked with Jerry?" to which Dean replied, "Yeah…but our stuff wasn't that funny, I'll tell you that." It was scenes such as that the audience waited for every week.

Dean continued to be a man of multiple careers. In addition to his weekly television show, he continued to record for Reprise and also made a dozen films in the nine years *The Dean Martin Show* was on the air. His roles included playing the spy Matt Helm in the 1966 American spy spoof film *The Silencers*. In three years, there would be three more films starring Dean as Matt Helm. The series was a smashing success. Incredibly, Dean made time every day to hit the links. Work could not keep him away from his true love of golf.

By the late 1960s, Dean was the highest paid entertainer in Hollywood, even making more than his pal, "The Chairman of the Board" himself, Sinatra. In 1967, NBC increased Dean's salary per episode from $44,000 to $283,000. The 3-year contract he signed was for $34 million. To add to his preeminent salary, Dean was the largest owner of RCA stock in history. Dean himself never cared much about money. His goal was to provide for his wife, children, and parents. Of course, having a little left over for play was a bonus. He was also richly rewarded for the show, picking up a Golden Globe in 1967 and being nominated three consecutive years.

There were no two people prouder of Dean than his parents, Guy and Angela. For Guy, an Italian immigrant turned barber in Steubenville, Ohio, to see his son at the top of the heap was overwhelming. He and Angela would be in the audience for Dean's show every week, though there were a few occasions when he would walk out because he claimed he had already seen that skit before. The Crocettis had come a long way from Ohio to Beverly Hills, and it was all thanks to their Dino.

Sadly, Christmas Day, 1966, was not a joyous Christmas for the Martin-Crocetti family. Dean's mother, Angela, died from bone cancer at the age of age of 69. Just eight months later, Guy followed his wife and passed away at 72. Dean was now without the two people who had given him the most love and support throughout his life and all of its ups and downs. There would be more loss still when one year after Guy died, Dean's only brother, Bill, was hospitalized with a brain tumor. There was nothing doctors could do for him, and Bill Crocetti died in October 1968 at only 52.

Dean threw himself more and more into work and his television show, continuing to have a rollicking time filming. Dean was performing with not only rising young stars such as Goldie Hawn, but also with legends such as Lucille Ball, Ella Fitzgerald, Jimmy Stewart, Orson Welles, and his personal idol, Harry Mills and The Mills Brothers. The most popular show was the 1967 "Dean Martin Christmas Show" featuring the Martin family, all seven children and Jeanne, and Frank and his three children. The special was one of the highest rated shows in NBC history.

Throughout the show's run, Dean's children made a few appearances of their own and were actively involved. His oldest son, Craig, became as associate producer and married one of "The Golddiggers." Gail, his second daughter, joined her father in a medley of songs, and Deana sang "You Are My Lucky Star" and "Side by Side" with her father. She also appeared in some skits on the show, as did Gail and her handsome brother, Dino. It appeared both Deana and Dino were on their way of following in their father's footsteps.

At home, the real Dean Martin was the opposite of the charismatic and boisterous man the public saw on television. They saw a man who appeared to enjoy his J & B scotch a bit too much and who relished the attention of beautiful women. The drinking was all a part of the act. Dean claimed the ever-present glass in his hand was only apple juice. But pretending it was scotch gave comics like Don Rickles an excuse to rib Dean about his Italian blood.

Even Jeanne gave Dean her approval of maintaining the act of drinking and being the ladies' man. Greg Garrison, who knew Dean for 30 years, claimed he never saw Dean go out on stage inebriated, and he never had to worry about it either. When asked by Dinah Shore if he really drank as much as was portrayed he said, "Do you think that NBC would put up millions of dollars for 15 years for a drunk that didn't study?"

Dean capitalized on his image of being a drunk in his stage performances and during the show. During a scene with Don Rickles depicting them in a western bar, Dean the cowboy tells the bartender he'll have a glass of milk. Not missing a cue, Dean says, "Are you sure this is my cue card?" Rickles jested back, "He should get an Academy Award for reading that line." Always insisting that was an image he cultivated on, the audience liked to see he was just a regular guy who enjoyed a drink. Part of the genius of Dean Martin was having the ability to read the audience.

6 DENOUEMENT

"He was shy. That's really what it was all about. He was a shy man. The performance came when the lights went on. Showtime!"

~ *Greg Garrison, Producer of* The Dean Martin Show

It is said one of the most endearing traits a performer can and should possess is a sense of humility, never forgetting one's roots. If that is the case, Dean Martin is a quintessential star who embodied humility throughout his career. What his peers loved most about him was his lack of ego. He was the highest paid entertainer in the industry but continued to treasure for praise.

On one occasion, the comedian Dom DeLuise complimented Dean on his performance of a song, telling him it was wonderful. Dean looked at him with a sort of gleam in his eye and asked, "Was it?" In his heart, he remained that Italian-American boy from Steubenville who was kidded for his way of dress, just looking for acceptance.

As he entered the 70s, Dean was still a blockbuster name at the box offices. In 1970, he appeared in director Ross Hunter's disaster-drama, *Airport*. Dean played airline captain Vernon Demarest with an all-star cast including Burt Lancaster, Helen Hayes, Van Heflin, Jacqueline Bisset, George Kennedy, and Maureen Stapleton. In addition to movies and television, Dean was also still a success in his nightclub act. At an age where men were slowing down, Dean was busier than ever.

Dean's hectic schedule and eye for beautiful younger women took a toll on his marriage to Jeanne. Dean had begun dating the 22-year-old 1969 First Runner Up in the Miss World contest, Gail Renshaw. Dean left Jeanne and moved out of the family home at 601 Mountain Drive in Beverly Hills. Jeanne agreed to divorce Dean. Though she still loved him, she acknowledged it was apparent he no longer felt the same about her.

While waiting for his divorce from Jeanne to finalize, Dean's relationship with Gail fizzled out after a brief engagement. In 1973, after 24 years of marriage, Dean and Jeanne were divorced. On April 26, 1973, Dean married an attractive young hair salon receptionist named Catherine Hawn. Dean was 55 and she was 25 with a 6-year-old daughter named Sasha, whom Dean adopted. Their honeymoon was over almost as soon as it began, and they divorced in 1976.

There were more endings ahead for Dean as his variety show's ratings plummeted. Finally, after trying to rejuvenate interest in the show, NBC cancelled *The Dean Martin Show* after nine years. But Dean would not be off of NBC for long. Part of NBC's scheme to bring the show's ratings up was to include a segment called "Man of the Week Celebrity Roast." The roasts consisted of having a celebrity on a dais surrounded by an entourage of peers "roasting" them, or mockingly adulating and insulting them for an hour. The idea derived from the roasts held at the New York Friars Club, where Dean made regular appearances.

The first "Man of the Week Celebrity Roast" aired in January 1973 on *The Dean Martin Show* and the honoree was *Tonight Show* host Johnny Carson. NBC noticed that the roasts were popular and widely anticipated, so they opted to pick up Dean and the roasts after his weekly show was cancelled. The first *Dean Martin Celebrity Roast* aired on Thursday, October 31, 1974, roasting comic legend Bob Hope.

Originally, the roasts were filmed on the NBC lot in Burbank but beginning in 1974, NBC moved Dean to the Ziegfeld Room at the MGM Grand Hotel in Las Vegas. For 10 years, with the exception of 1980-1983 when the MGM Grand was under reconstruction after a calamitous fire, *The Dean Martin Celebrity Roast* was held in the Ziegfeld Room and was the most awaited program on television.

"The Man of the Hour" and "The Woman of the Hour" run the gamut from politicians to celebrities to sports heroes. Famous "Roastees" included: Lucille Ball, Jackie Gleason, Betty White, Frank Sinatra, Jimmy Stewart, Wilt Chamberlain, Muhammad Ali, Joe Namath, Senator Barry Goldwater of Arizona, former vice president Hubert Humphrey, and Governor Ronald Reagan of California. Even the Founding Father of the United States himself, George Washington, was roasted posthumously. Jan

Leighton, a historical impersonator, portrayed Washington, and Audrey Meadows appeared as Martha.

Viewers soon came to know and love regular "Roasters" on the show such as: Don Rickles, Nipsy Russell, Ruth Buzzi, Phyllis Diller, Red Buttons, and Foster Brooks, who always portrayed an inebriate slurring his words. And of course, there was the beloved "Roast Master" who presided over the dais – with the exception of when he was roasted – Dean Martin. It seemed America could never get enough of Dean.

The pinnacle and highlight of Dean's latter career came in a moment that few foresaw, including Dean. Beginning in 1966, Jerry Lewis played host to the annual MDA (Muscular Dystrophy Association) Labor Day Telethon, occasionally bringing on famous friends like Frank Sinatra to lend their support. In 1976, Frank decided that the telethon was the perfect place to reunite the two men who had once held the title of the most famous duo in America.

Dean agreed to do it, and Jerry stood in shock and emotion as Frank brought his old friend and partner out onto the stage. The two men embraced and wiped tears from their eyes. It was the first time they had spoken in 20 years. Jerry later said of the unforgettable occasion, "It was the thrill of my life having him stand there next to me." The reconciliation was also a beautiful moment for the millions of fans who had been waiting two decades for the pair to reunite.

In 1980, Frank and Dean reunited to embark on a campaign tour for their old pal, Ronald Reagan. Dean never had a strong interest in politics like Frank, but in the 60s he had been a part of the Democrats for Reagan coalition that Frank headed. He genuinely liked and respected Ronald Reagan and believed him to be the best candidate. In 1985, when then President Reagan was honored by his Hollywood cohorts at "An All-Star Tribute to Ronald Reagan" in Burbank, Dean serenaded the room with a hysterical version of "Mr. Wonderful."

After Dean's celebrity roasts went off NBC in 1984, he went back to his one-man nightclub act in Vegas. According to close friends, Dean felt unneeded after he went off the air regularly. After being at the top for so many years, the decline was steep. Dean would always say he needed to work because he had a large family to provide for, and the family always came first, but the truth was he loved to work. The work gave him a purpose, and without it, that purpose dwindled. When asked in 1983 if he planned on retiring, he shook his head, saying, "When you retire, you die. You've got to get up to something. You can't get up…to nothing."

He found comfort in his personal life again. Years after their divorce, he and Jeanne found companionship again, though they never remarried. Dean went to London in 1983 to perform at the Palladium, and Jeanne accompanied him on the tour, along with their youngest daughter, Gina. Jeanne remembered his performance as being wonderful, but strenuous, and he returned home exhausted. She had always been there for Dean and was there to hold his hand during what would be the most difficult time in both of their lives.

On March 21, 1987, Dean and Jeanne received word that their son, Captain Dean Paul Martin, Jr., had disappeared along with the crew of the F-4C Phantom jet fighter he was navigating. Dino's passion since childhood had been flying, and now he was serving the California National Guard. For five days Dean held out hope that his son may be found alive, but in her heart, Jeanne knew he was gone. The wreckage of the plane was discovered on her birthday. Dino Martin had vanished into the San Bernardino Mountains. He was 35 years-old and left a 12-year-old son, Alex, behind. His father was shattered.

After a memorial service at Los Angeles National Cemetery, Dean was at home speaking to his closest friend and agent, Mort Viner. Mort told him he noticed Jerry Lewis slip into the back row during the service. Touched and surprised to hear his old partner had come, he asked Mort to get him on the phone. His call to Jerry to tell him thank you turned into a two-hour conversation. In 1989, the duo appeared on stage together for what would be the last time in Las Vegas to celebrate Dean's 72nd birthday. 40 years later, the chemistry and love were still evident.

Dean's friends were worried about the usually energetic and charismatic Dean after the death of Dean Paul. Frank Sinatra saw his pal slipping into a depression and schemed up the idea of bringing him, Dean, and Sammy back together again. Fittingly, the reunion was titled, "Together Again." The show opened in Oakland in March 1988 to a sold-out crowd coming to see that old Rat Pack magic once again, more than likely for the last time.

At 72, Sinatra's voiced had aged, but he still sang with the same gusto he had when he was 30, Sammy had his usual energy and jazz, but Dean appeared to be frail and lacking in zest. He had the occasional charm but his heart was never in the performance, and he left the group after six shows. Dean returned to his show in Las Vegas while Sammy and Frank continued the tour, adding Liza Minnelli to the billing and retitling it "The Ultimate Event." The days of the Rat Pack were over.

7 SWEET, SWEET MEMORIES

*"Dean was my brother – not through blood but through choice.
Our friendship has traveled down many roads over the years,
and there will always be a special place in my heart and soul for
Dean. He has been like the air I breathe – always there,
always close by."*

~ Frank Sinatra

From the late 1980s into the 1990s, those who witnessed Dean perform his show in Vegas did not recognize the man who was known for his energy and zest for making his audience laugh. Now he was over 70, forgetting his lines, and his whole performance seemed to be forced. His jokes about drinking and getting drunk had run their course of being funny. Now they were just sad.

In September 1991, Dean hung up his microphone and retired from performing. Though he was still a popular performer and loved all around the world, it was clear his fans did not want to witness the decline of Dean Martin. However, Dean did not entirely give up the limelight. He would do anything for a friend or one of his children. When daughter Deana asked her father to appear in a commercial for her fitness center in Beverly Hills, no one was more surprised to hear him say yes than she was. Like any good father, he could not turn his daughter down.

Aging was not easy for Dean. Not only was he dealing with bodily pains and the loss of activities he enjoyed, such as golf, he was also watching as friends from his good old days passed away one by one. In May of 1990, Sammy Davis, Jr. died after a battle with cancer. Upon the death of his old friend, Dean released a statement saying, "As great an entertainer as Sammy was, he was even a greater friend." Sammy, nicknamed "Smokey," was the first of the timeless trio to go.

After retiring from Vegas, Dean became a virtual recluse in declining health. For years, he had struggled with dental problems, exasperated by his love of sugar, alcohol, and tobacco. The pain that resulted from the oral surgeries led to a strong reliance on painkillers that Dean found hard to give up. His bad back had caused him to give up his favorite pastime of golf, but he still shot some pool at his Beverly Hills home. Perhaps worst of all, Dean began losing his eyesight. Of all his ailments in his final years, it was the loss of vision that affected him the most.

Restricting himself to his home and bedroom, Dean spent the majority of his day in his pajamas, lying in bed watching television. He especially loved *Jeopardy!* In the evenings, Dean would be driven down to his favorite restaurant on Santa Monica Boulevard, Da Vinci. There, he would sit alone and eat while passersby would exclaim, "There's Dean Martin!" On

Sundays, he would haunt another favorite joint on Sunset Boulevard, the Hamburger Hamlet. His family, which now included numerous grandchildren, would stop by and visit him, and once a week he dined alone with Jeanne. More than love, there was a strong bond between the two that never dissipated.

When Dean would venture out of his home, paparazzi was sure to be there. They took every opportunity they could to get a picture of the aging Dean, once capturing him leaving Da Vinci without his teeth in. The last images the public saw of him were under aggrandized headlines such as, "Dean Martin's Tragic Last Days." For a man who had dedicated 50 years to entertaining and making others happy, he deserved more respect and dignity in his last months.

Dean's last public appearance was when he called into *Geraldo* in 1994 when Deana was appearing with other children of well-known entertainers. Geraldo asked him about Frank, Jerry, and his health. Geraldo ended the phone conversation by asking Dean what he had to say to Deana. He replied, "To my Deana? Just that I love her. I always will love her, I always have, and that's about it. She's the sweetest gal I know." For a man who juggled so many projects in entertainment, he did a remarkable job of keeping his large family together and his children adored him. It was a bittersweet ending to his career.

Dean Martin breathed his last around 3:30 a.m. on Christmas morning, 1995. He was 78 years-old, and the official cause was acute respiratory failure. Ironically, he died 29 years to the day his mother Angela had passed away in 1966. At 7:00 p.m., Las Vegas dimmed the lights along the strip for one minute to remember Dean. The only person before Dean to receive such an honor was Sammy. The family held a private service on December 28 in the chapel at Westwood Village Memorial Park. He was interred in a mausoleum not far from his parents and close to his old friend, Marilyn Monroe. On his crypt are the words to the song he made immortal, "Everybody Loves Somebody Sometime."

Dean was asked during an interview toward the end of his career how he would like to be remembered as a performer. His answer: "As a damn good entertainer. That's about it. Nothing spectacular...They'll remember me." A man of few words, nothing he said could have been truer. In the years following his death, Dean's popularity has continued to rise, thanks to his timeless music, the pride of his hometown, and the continuation of his legacy through his children. His son, Ricci, performed a show for almost 10 years called *His Son Remembers: Dean Martin's Music and More*. Deana has spent years performing her father's songs in concert and in the studio, releasing albums such as *Memories Are Made of This* and *Volare*.

The last years of the twentieth century saw the end of the Rat Pack. In November 1996, the Sands Hotel in Las Vegas, where Dean, Frank, Sammy, Joey, and Peter, had all left their footprints as the biggest performers in Sin City in the 60s, was demolished. Then, in May 1998, Frank Sinatra died at the age of 82, the last of the famous three of the Rat Pack. Though all three were gone, their legacies continued to explode into the new millennium.

Steubenville, Ohio, had always been proud of the native son who put their city on a map. Throughout his career, Dean never shied in talking about where he came from and how his roots had grounded him. Working in the mills would forever ingratiate in him the appreciation and utmost respect for the hard workers who barely made enough to support their families. When he was the highest paid entertainer in the industry, he incessantly gave to local charities and family members in Steubenville.

In 1996, Steubenville rightly decided to honor their hometown hero. On June 7, 1996, what would have been his 79th birthday, the first Dean Martin Festival was held. The festival consisted of Dean impersonators, as well as some Sammy and Frank, auctions of Dean Martin memorabilia, and many more "Dean" activities and festivities. A few years into the festival, Deana made a surprise appearance and, in her book, recounted how overwhelmed at the thousands of people who showed up because of their love for her father. Crowds bundled around "just to touch her."

As if the Dean Martin Festival was not enough to pay tribute to the legend himself, there was soon talk of establishing a "Dean Martin Day" in Ohio. For two years there were discussions back and forth in the state senate about changing the law in Ohio for an official Dean Day to be declared. Finally the bill was brought to the floor and passed in 2002. On June 7, Ohio honors the man born Dino Paul Crocetti in Steubenville, who became the one and only Dean Martin. To add to the commemoration, the post office issued a commemorative stamp in his honor.

Dean Martin the entertainer is easy to sum up. His appeal is everlasting because of the deep sound of romance that radiates from his crooning voice, his impeccable way of dressing, with a drink and cigarette always in his hand, and his infectious sense of humor and dashing white smile set against a deep tan. Joey Bishop remembered Dean as being the most honest performer he ever saw perform, and the audience sensed that honesty.

Greg Garrison said of his friend of more than 30 years that he was the most kind and gentle human being he knew, never causing a ruckus or complaining about life or work. For years after Dean's death, Jerry would become emotional discussing his old partner, but he always gave Dean the credit he so deserved, saying, "We had a genius in our midst, unrecognized, probably unfulfilled, and more than likely the most underrated greatest straight man that ever lived." He reminisced on their years together and apart in a 2005 book, *Dean and Me: A Love Story*.

The real Dean is more difficult to understand. To his family, he was always an enigma. Even Jeanne, who knew him better than anyone, said she never really knew the man she spent more than 40 years with. She claimed what most people did not know about Dean was that he hated to talk, conversation did not come naturally to him. His ideal day would be sitting in a small motel room with a television watching westerns by himself. A mirror opposite of the Dean on television, his family and friends knew that was all a performance, but that was what made him a brilliant entertainer.

Angie Dickinson, one of Dean's oldest friends, said of Dean, "Something in his psyche didn't allow us to come in and see the real Dean." For a man who spent so many years in the spotlight, he said very little about his private life and remained reserved. Often,

41

the funniest of people bear the prickliest of thorns through life. Perhaps that was the case with Dean and the reason for his reserved personality.

America and the world fell in love with Dean. They felt they knew him. To the public, he was so familiar; he was in their homes, at the movies, and singing in the Italian restaurants they ate in. Dean was and still is everywhere. As long as there is music in the air, romance, and laughter, yes Dean, you will be remembered.

We hope you enjoyed reading this book as much as we enjoyed creating it. If you did, the team would greatly appreciate your feedback on Amazon or your favorite forum.

Please sign up for the LearningList at in60Learning.com to receive free ebooks, audiobooks, and updates on our new releases.

Happy reading!

The in60Learning Team

Made in United States
North Haven, CT
21 December 2021

13392576R00029